BOOK
4
All-American Series

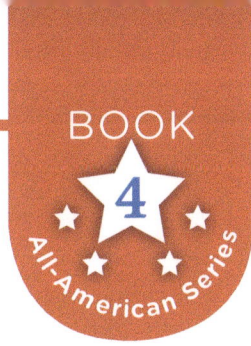

Victory
at the Vet's

By Gene & Bobbie Carnell

© 2017 by innerQuest, an imprint of Chiron Publications. All rights reserved. No part of this publication may be reproduced, stored in a retrieval system, or transmitted, in any form by any means, electronic, mechanical, photocopying, recording, or otherwise, without the prior written permission of the publisher, Chiron Publications, 932 Hendersonville Road, Suite 104, Asheville, North Carolina 28803.

innerQuestBooks.com
ChironPublicatons.com

innerQuest is a book imprint of Chiron Publications
Edited by Jennifer Fitzgerald
Interior and cover design by Lisa Alford
Printed primarily in the United States of America.

If you are an organization wishing to buy bulk quantities of this book, please contact Chiron Publications at generalmanager@chironpublications.com

ISBN 978-1-63051-436-5 paperback

Library of Congress Cataloging-in-Publication Data Pending

Art courtesy of Freepik.com, Creative Commons, and the New York Public Library Digital Collection

Dedicated to those in the healing
profession who extend care and compassion
to humans and animals alike–
thank you!

All-American Series

We Americans have always had a love affair with animals—from "Animal Crackers" to the Detroit Lions and the Chicago Bears! We tend to imagine them having human-like qualities. This may be because these incredible creatures often become our good friends. Maybe we enjoy them so much because they seem to love us without asking anything in return.

They are glad to simply share our lives with us. But they look to us to provide for them and protect them from hurt or cruelty.

I hope you have a pet or two. Taking care of them teaches us responsibility while giving us lots of pleasure.

Here is a story about VICTORY, our national bird, and how he was helped and healed. I think you will like hearing it because it turned out so well.

Uncle Sam

One morning Missy, our beautiful Siamese cat, appeared to Aunt Samantha and me to be very sick. She had not eaten for a couple of days and she was very quiet.

Aunt Samantha called the vet later that morning and I was told that I was supposed to pick up some medicine for her on the way to work.

When I entered the vet's office just outside of Washington, D.C., the waiting room was already full of pet-patients and their owners. I saw two kinds of vets that morning. In case you were wondering there are two very different kinds of vets.

VETS WHO ARE VETERANS—military men and women who have served in the Armed Forces—and VETERINARIANS who doctor sick animals, like our good friend Dr. Joan at her clinic.

There are "vets" who fought in the war to protect our freedom, and "vets" who fight disease and protect our furry and feathered friends.

I spoke, of course, to everyone including the doc, who was going around assuring everyone she would see them just as soon as she could.

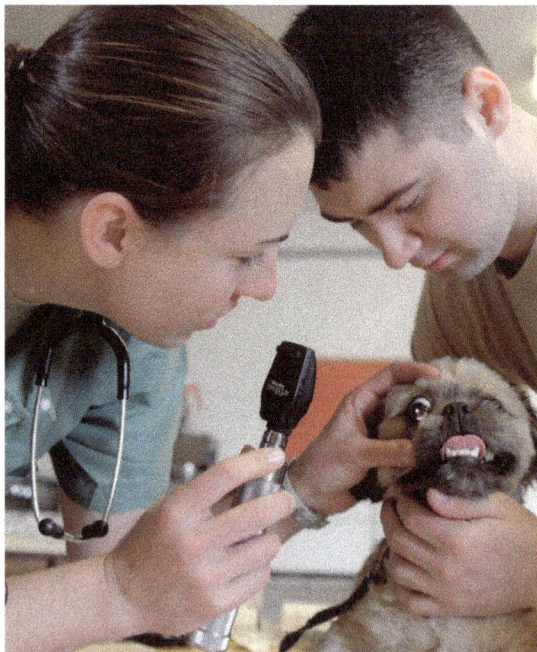

I could tell it was more than just another routine day at the office.

She instructed her receptionist to get the medicine for Missy, then disappeared beyond the swinging door that led to the back.

A nurse stepped in to announce, "Okay, Bugle Boy, we're ready for you." A lady rose from her chair, carrying her basset hound toward that same door and disappeared. He was a beautiful dog!

Just as I was getting ready to leave, the front door burst open. A man in a uniform carrying a lump of feathers in his arms called out, "I'm sorry to barge in folks, but our national mascot, 'VICTORY' the eagle is very sick. I'm afraid he may die. Where's the vet?"

Everyone crowded around trying to see. Some tried to help, expressing concern.

A lady sitting near me said, "Oh, go right ahead, take our spot," holding her poodle tightly. "Our problem can wait." The lady pointed to the swinging door. "She's back there!"

"Yes, by all means," another lady chimed in. "Fifi is only having her regular check-up—and a shampoo."

The uniformed man appeared to be a member of the White House Security Police and interrupted. "You say she's back there?" He rushed through that door.

As you can imagine, everyone was talking among themselves. It was noisy and confusing. I noticed a small girl in the corner that seemed to be very upset.

In a moment, things quieted down and this little girl, about 6 or 7 years old, who was sitting with an elderly lady, began to speak softly, "Oh Grandma, I'm worried and really scared."

"Now, Sarah, honey, don't you fret. We've come through a lot of hard times in this country by sticking together. We'll get through this crisis, too. Dr. Joan is an excellent doctor, you'll see."

Another lady across from them added, "Yes, I've been through some difficult times, too. I lost my husband many years ago in World War II. I thought I'd never make it, but faith and friends brought me out. 'Victory' is our national emblem and is important to the morale of our country."

A gentleman on the other side of the room, trying to cheer up Sarah said, "I'm sure they'll do all they can to cure him. Would you like to pet my puppy? He loves pretty girls like you."

By now I must admit, I was getting a little concerned, but as I looked around and listened, I became encouraged. Something good was happening here!

Slipping out of my seat, I walked over to where they were, knelt down and asked, "Grandma, may I talk with Sarah a moment?"

"Of course, I know you!" Grandma replied.

"Sarah, let me tell you a story about another famous and special eagle. It happened many years ago during the Civil War. A Native American in the northern woods of Wisconsin found a small eaglet that had fallen out of a tree."

"He fed it fish and meat and it soon became tame. He was a Chippewa chief named 'Blue Sky.' He eventually sold the eagle to a white man for 5 bushels of corn because his people were hungry."

"The 8th Wisconsin Volunteers thought it would be fine to take a real live 'Bird of Freedom' to the war, so they bought it for $2.50."

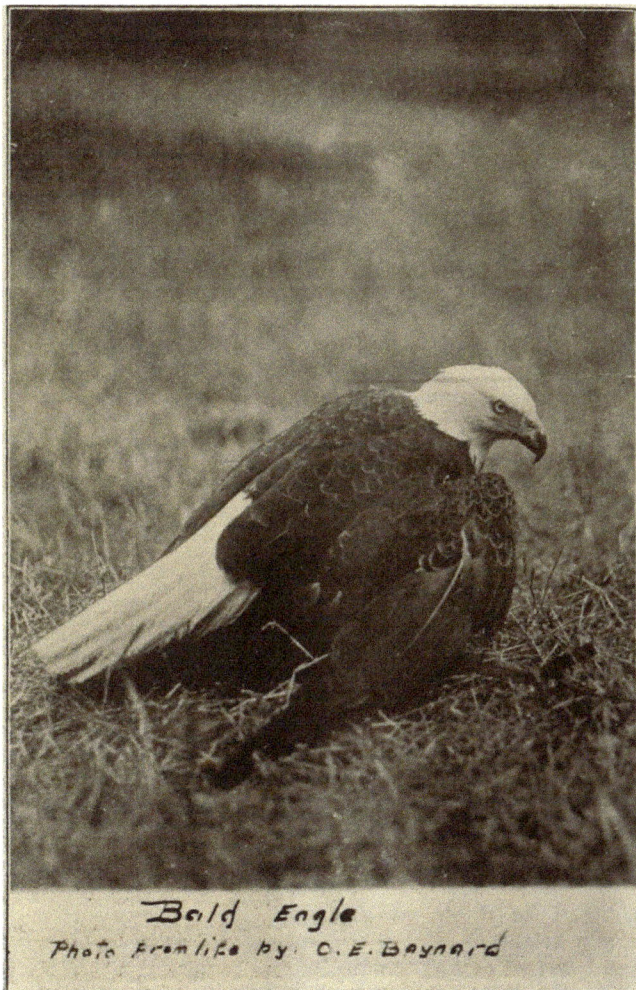

Bald Eagle
Photo from life by. C. E. Baynard

"The eagle, now full grown, strutted around camp and like a dog, it chose a master and friend. He was a young Irish soldier named Jimmie McGinnis who would not allow anyone else to feed the eagle."

"Really?" Sarah whispered, her face brightening.

"Yes, this is a true story. Well, Jimmie made a red, white and blue shield for the eagle's perch. He set the shield on a pole and tied the eagle by the foot so he could not fly away. When the regiment went on march, Jimmie carried him beside the color bearer. The eagle was cheered by crowds of people in every town."

"He was named 'Old Abe' for President Lincoln because the eagle seemed to have the same determination. And he loved marching with the soldiers and music."

Others crowded close to listen. "But battles excited him. The first time he heard a cannon shot, he broke his cord and flew away."

"The soldiers thought he was gone forever. When the battle was over, he returned to his friend Jimmie, and his perch."

"After that, 'Old Abe' was not tied anymore. He often flew off to go hunting or fishing. The soldiers always welcomed him when he came back into camp."

"That eagle went through four years of war, 22 battles in all, and after every battle he returned to his own regiment. He was often hit by flying bullets that tore his feathers, but he was never badly hurt."

"And listen to this folks: When the war was over, 'Old Abe' was given to the state of Wisconsin. For 15 years, he lived at the State House in Madison, the capitol. Jimmie remained his friend and keeper the whole time."

"Sarah, I believe that our 'Victory' has some of the same good qualities and strength. He has already survived a lot and I just feel like he's going to come through this too. We must have hope and believe in it. Will you try to do that with us?"

Sarah, eyes beaming, said "Okay, Uncle Sam, I will," for her grandmother had explained to her who the kindly gentleman talking with her really was.

"What about the rest of you folks?"

They said in unison, "We will too!"

A business-type looking man holding a large macaw who was chattering "United We Stand!" "United We Stand!" said, "Our family lost two nephews fighting in the Korean War and a grandson in the Vietnam War.

"You don't know how strong you can be until you've been put to the test. This country is full of folks who are glad to help somebody when they are in trouble. Just look at how September 11th brought us all together."

Several people nodded their heads in silent agreement.

I called Aunt Samantha on my cell phone to tell her the situation. Soon she came in, greeted everyone, and asked what she could do to help. Knowing how good she was with animals, I suggested that she go back to assist them. The nurse agreed and led her through that same door while all of us watched and waited.

Soon, she and Dr. Joan came back, along with the guard. Dr. Joan said, "Now don't worry, I don't see anything seriously wrong with Victory. Leave him here overnight and we'll evaluate him again in the morning."

At that, her receptionist tried to brighten the mood, "Mrs. Alexander, your Precious and her babies are next."

Stroking the tiny ball of fluff, the doc apologized again. "I am very sorry to keep you all waiting."

"That's no problem, we understand, don't we?" the grandmother smiles.

A young man across the room supports her, saying, "No we don't mind at all. It's important to get our national symbol well again."

The doc replied, "Well, he is very old but seems strong."

Then the young man asked, "Could we come back tomorrow and see how he is in the morning?"

"Yes! Yes!" they all said.

Dr. Joan responded, "Of course. Thanks again for your kindness and patience."

After sleeping very little that night and feeling anxious about Victory's chance and condition, we all met the next morning at the vet's office.

The waiting room was more crowded than before. The news had spread! There were firemen, policemen, school children and just everyday citizens, even some without pets who were curious and concerned.

When we walked in, everyone spoke to us warmly. One lady said, "Oh, I surely hope our eagle is alright."

The grandmother was back with Sarah and said, "Sarah and I prayed for him last night."

The man with the macaw echoed, "We're all pulling for him. It's the American way!"

The receptionist interrupted, "There's coffee and juice for you over on the counter.

"Please sit down and relax. We'll let you know something very soon."

Then she escorted Aunt Samantha and me back through the door to meet with the doctor—where we heard the good news!

In just a few minutes, we all came back in with Victory perched pertly on my arm, alive and well—and as sassy as ever.

Everyone stood and applauded as I told them, "Folks, the doc says he's as good as new."

"What did you do Dr. Joan?" the crowd replied. "Yes, tell us."

The doctor said, "Actually not very much. It's kind of hard to explain medically. I think it has more to do with what took place out here than in the treatment room."

Aunt Samantha asked, "Really? What do you mean?"

"I mean, from what I saw. The attitude of kindness, cooperation, unselfishness and concern for his safety probably did the most good. You folks putting his well-being ahead of your own problems may be the key."

"I believe you are right," Aunt Samantha agreed. "These qualities are good medicine for people, much less our animals. These kinds of actions are what makes a nation strong. I'm sure Uncle Sam will agree."

"Absolutely!" I said. "And let me thank each one of you for your thoughtfulness you have showed towards Victory. I'm very proud of you—all of you!"

"It's when we are joined in purpose that really makes us better as a people. When we rally around one another in support and love, miracles really can happen."

People stood and formed little groups to the side as they congratulated the doctor, her staff and one another.

It seemed as if everyone was trying to talk at the same time. But it was a happy sound—not confusing or alarming. And it was apparent they were in no hurry to leave, although many of them had appointments and jobs to go to.

So, I spoke up again and said, "Since you all have been such good cheerleaders, let me lead you in one before we all go, alright?"

"Yeah, great!"

"Let's do it!"

"Right on!"

"Okay then, let's stand together."

They stood in an orderly fashion pushing the chairs back to make room. Joining hands, they awaited my signal.

I said, "GIVE ME AN A!" The crowd responded, "A!"

"GIVE ME AN M!" And again, "M!"

"GIVE ME AN E!" They shouted, "E!"

"GIVE ME AN R!" And again, they shouted, "R!"

"GIVE ME AN I!" In unison, "I!"

"GIVE ME A C!" Again, "C!"

"GIVE ME ANOTHER A!" an enthusiastic, thunderous response, "A!"

"What does that spell?—AMERICA!"

"I can't hear you!" - more boldly, loudly and clearly—"AMERICA!"

"MAY GOD BLESS—AMERICA" as one.

Amid cheers, applause, hugs and handshakes, we Americans scattered and went about our individual business—for life goes on!

It was a very special day and something we don't think we'll ever forget. And, oh yes, Missy was alright too.

> "FOR WHAT AVAIL THE PLOUGH OR SAIL,
> OR LAND OR LIFE, IF FREEDOM FAIL?"
> - RALPH WALDO EMERSON

AMERICA the BEAUTIFUL
(Words by Katherine Lee Bates...Music by Samuel A. Ward)

A trip to Pike's Peak in 1893, inspired poetess Katherine Bates to write these patriotic lines. It was a hard wagon drive through the heat and thin air to the top, but the view provided an incredible feast for her eyes. Miss Bates remarked, "It is not work to write a song; it is a great joy."

O beautiful for spacious skies, for amber waves of grain.

For purple mountain majesty, above the fruited plain.

A-mer-i-ca! A-mer-i-ca! God shed His grace on thee, and

crown thy good with brotherhood, from sea to shining sea.

O beautiful for patriot dream, that sees beyond the years.

Thine alabaster cities gleam, undimmed by human tears.

A-mer-i-ca! A-mer-i-ca! God shed His grace on thee, and

crown thy good with brotherhood, from sea to shining sea.

LESSONS FOR LIFE

1. Be cautious of folks who mistreat animals
2. There are rewards even when we sacrifice (do without).
3. Doing good results in feeling good.
4. To have a friend, be a friend.
5. Self-respect is always satisfying.

www.ingramcontent.com/pod-product-compliance
Lightning Source LLC
Chambersburg PA
CBHW051310020426
42331CB00018B/3492